BLACKBIRD

14

A

2020

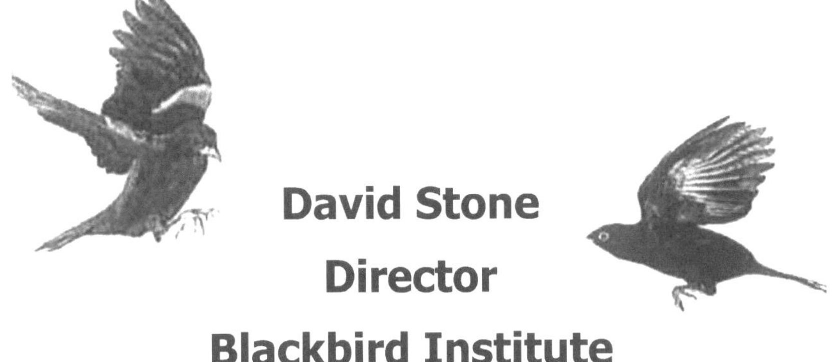

David Stone

Director

Blackbird Institute

ARTISTS

Darlene Altschul	USA
Alwina	Great Britain
David Aponte	USA
Eric Basso	USA
Michael Begnal	USA
Harry Burrus	Mexico
Alan Catlin	USA
David Chirot	USA
McArthur Gunter	USA
Wolfgang Guenther	Germany
Faith Heisler	USA
Eberhard Janke	Germany
Dob Kamperelic	Serbia
Bob Kim	USA
Solamito Luigino	Italy
Rita McNamara	USA
Ruggero Maggi	Italy
Mailarta	Canada
Nemacka	Serbia
Katerina Nikoltsou (with Carolyn Cline)	Greece
Andrew Niss	Germany
Normal	USA
Cheryl Penn	South Africa
Nadia-Cella Pop	Romania
Arpad Salamon	Slovenia
Dennis Saleh	USA
Dan Setzer	USA
LaVona Sherarts	USA
Arnold Skemer	USA
Judy Skolnick	USA

David Stone	USA
Marilyn Stone	USA
Giovanni Strada	Italy
Bart Verburg	Netherlands
Guido Vermuelen	Belgium
Mindaugaz Zuromskas	Lithuania
Mike Dyar	USA
Teresinka Pereira	USA

Acknowledgements

Thanks to Harry Burrus for title page, editor's bio, Dob's memorial and back cover. Thanks to Cheryl Penn for front cover, and Jessica memorial. Thanks to Dan Setzer for Basso memorial. Cheryl Penn's 'Babel'-Edition 2 and 'Unfinished Book'-'Letters to Spring'. David

Stone's CITADEL poetry has been previously published in Pense Aqui,ZYX, Angel Fire Art and The Encyclopedia of Everything; Parts I-IV have been published by Cyberwit.net.

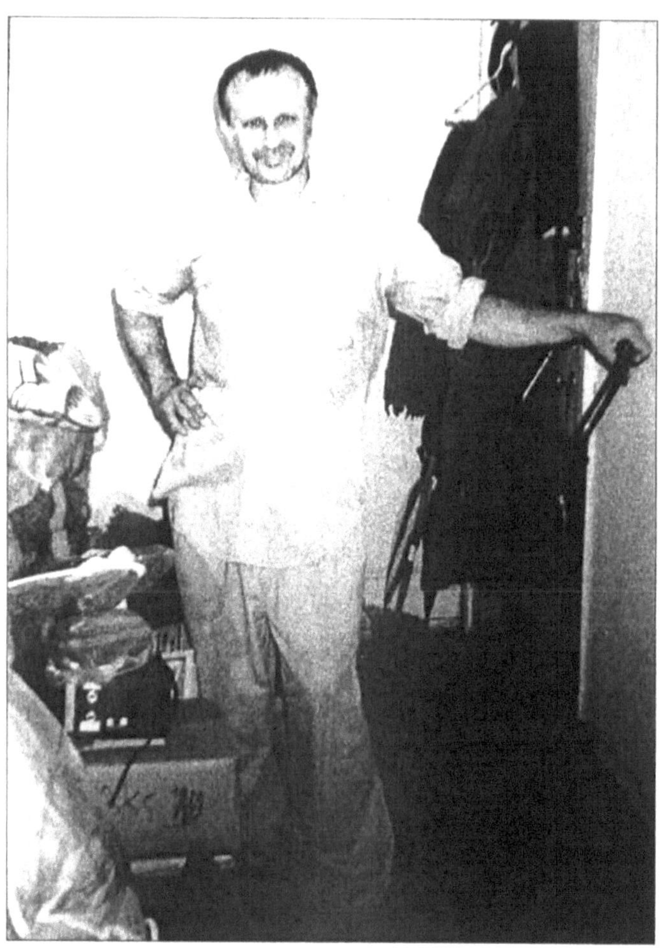

David Stone moves critical archives on a sweltering Baltimore day

David Stone hails from the Midwest. He experienced his early walking days in Chicago. He graduated from the University of Illinois with a degree in Philosophy and continues to have a strong philosophical curiosity and remains an avid reader of the subject. He participates in international mail art and enjoys translating, most recently Serbian poetry. He works on his writing every day, often at the One World Café in Baltimore. He publishes Blackbird, a literary-art publication.

By David Stone

Poetry
Specular Shards 1998
The Dark Ship Eclipse 1994
The joking Muse 1995
The Bridge Poems 2007
The Crystal Prism 2014
The Memory Strait 2016
The Citadel 2018
Citadel Vol. 2 2019

Fiction
The Find 1995

For available book titles, back issues of Blackbird, and poetry booklets
inquire by email: chocozzz2@aol.com:

ERIC BASSO DEDICATION

I first encountered Eric Basso when I found THE GOLEM TRIPTYCH on a bookshelf at The People's Bookstore in Milwaukee in 1996. My reaction was that this is the best work of American drama that I have ever seen. Knowing Basso now as well as I do, he would appreciate that reaction but take issue with my classification. He is more European in his outlook as a writer. When I moved to Baltimore and sent out invitations to contribute poetry and art to the first issue of Blackbird from the list of contributors in Harry Burrus' 0!!Zone, Eric responded immediately with a large supply of poetry that matched the flavor of the project which supplied many issues. We became good friends, meeting several times every year since then for enjoyable dinner or after dinner meetings, sometimes in groups, sometimes the two of us. His work has graced every issue of Blackbird and his loss is deeply felt by many. He has enriched literature with his poetry, drama, fiction and prose. His knowledge of history was astonishingly broad and deep. He had a sharp with a humorous touch and a deep compassion for humanity combined with a stark realism. I am grateful that Eric Basso touched my life, enriched my knowledge of history and literature and the many issues of Blackbird to which he contributed.

David Stone
June 18, 2019

Suddenly, on June 10, 2019 an extraordinary voice in contemporary literature fell silent.

Eric Basso was a poet, raconteur, novelist, playwright and critic. Eric leaves behind a huge body of work. His most popular works are the novella, "The Beak Doctor," and the cycle of three plays entitled, "The Golem Triptych."

Eric was born in 1947. His parents were devout Catholics, and made sure that he had the best possible Catholic education under the watchful eyes of the Jesuits. As a result, Eric became vehemently anticlerical, and remained so for the rest of his life.

In 1966 he entered Catonsville Community College. The college was new, and only recently accredited. As a result the school had difficulty recruiting top-notch, first-line professors. The school had to take what they could get, and what they got were instructors who were a collection of alcoholics, socially awkward misfits, trouble-making radicals and foreigners with accents so strong they could barely be understood.

Eric flourished in this environment. Even if the instructors showed up in class drunk or hung-over, they were brilliant, creative and fully engaged with the students. The foreign professors had multiple degrees earned in Europe, and filled important positions in their home counties before the Nazi's came. During the war they entered the underground resistance, and had an understanding of international affairs during the Cold War that was uncommon for the more sheltered Americans.

Eric made many friends at Catonsville who remained close friends for the rest of his life.

After completing community college he moved on to Towson State College (now University) in 1968. This is where I first met him, and we hit it off immediately. I found his sharp, acerbic wit, and encyclopedic knowledge of history and literature irresistible.

The Autumn of 1968 was a turbulent time in America. The Vietnam war was building to a crescendo, the Hippies were protesting the war, the struggle for civil rights was reaching a boiling point, and there was the ever-present threat of total annihilation from the Soviets during the Cold War.

The wider social circle of a full college resulted in a mad whorl of parties, skipped classes and carousing. We had so much fun that at the end of the semester our grades were so bad that we were asked to leave.

Getting kicked out of college gave us even more time for parties and carousing. But we also had more time to spend in book stores, intense reading, and long conversations about art and literature that often extended into the early morning hours.

We eventually went back to college and without the social distractions of that madcap semester Eric did brilliantly in his studies. In most cases I am sure that he brought more to the class than the professors.

Eric had incredible mental recall about everything he read. He told one story about being in a restaurant with friends when the conversation turned to some event in history. Eric began holding forth on the topic. An elderly lady approached the dinner table and placed a shinny new quarter on the table in front of Eric. She said, "I used to be a history teacher, and this is for you - for remembering all of the dates."For all his intellectual brilliance, Eric also had the amazing quality of being able to converse with anyone about anything without making them feel inferior. People from all stations in life felt comfortable talking to him.

Eric was also devoted to his huge Italian family. Whenever Eric was in the room there was laughter, and Eric remembered every funny or interesting story that happened to anyone in the family, and was always ready to tell those stories when the topic came up.

When his mother took ill, Eric forsook his writing for over five years to devote himself to her care and comfort. He never left her side, even relying on friends to buy his groceries and run his errands outside the home,

Artistically, Eric Basso's work defies classification. It can not be called Avant-Garde because that implies an artist who is in the forefront leading others into the unknown. Basso was not clearing a path for others to follow, he had no interest in starting a movement. Speculative Fiction doesn't fit either. It implies an artist who is trying out new approaches to see what will work.

Eric always had a very clear vision as to where he wanted to lead his readers, and with the sure hand of a master he realized that vision. Eric takes his readers to a strange land where ambiguity and uncertainty reign. His poetry paints images of momentous events of uncertain significance, that leave the reader questioning the fabric of his own reality.

As Eric published his books of fiction, and poetry he generously shared them with his friends and family. However, even his closest friends found his works to be mystifying and impenetrable. We would joke about it and tease him, demanding that he write something more accessible. "Eric, you are so witty, write something funny, just like you talk!"

Eric always took the jibes good-naturally, but remained steadfastly true to his vision and never gave in to the temptation to write accessible works that would garner him praise from la foule.

His critical works on the other hand were crystal clear. In his collection of critical essays, "Decompositions" Basso revealed relationships between the most disparate of facts and individuals that the rest of the world had missed.

That voice has fallen silent but he has left us with an incredible body of work that will take a generation to evaluate and to understand. As I grow older and re-read Eric's work, I find that I am beginning to get a glimmer of what he was trying to tell us. His work is very challenging, but very rewarding for the mature reader who takes the time to delve into the unique, strange, disquieting world that he has created. Once there, we are forced to draw disquieting conclusions about the so-called real world that we live in.

The voice has fallen silent, but Eric always knew that one day it would, and ordered that on his gravestone the words should be inscribed:

LITTERA SCRIPTA MANET
from Horace: "The Written Word Remains"

Dan Setzer

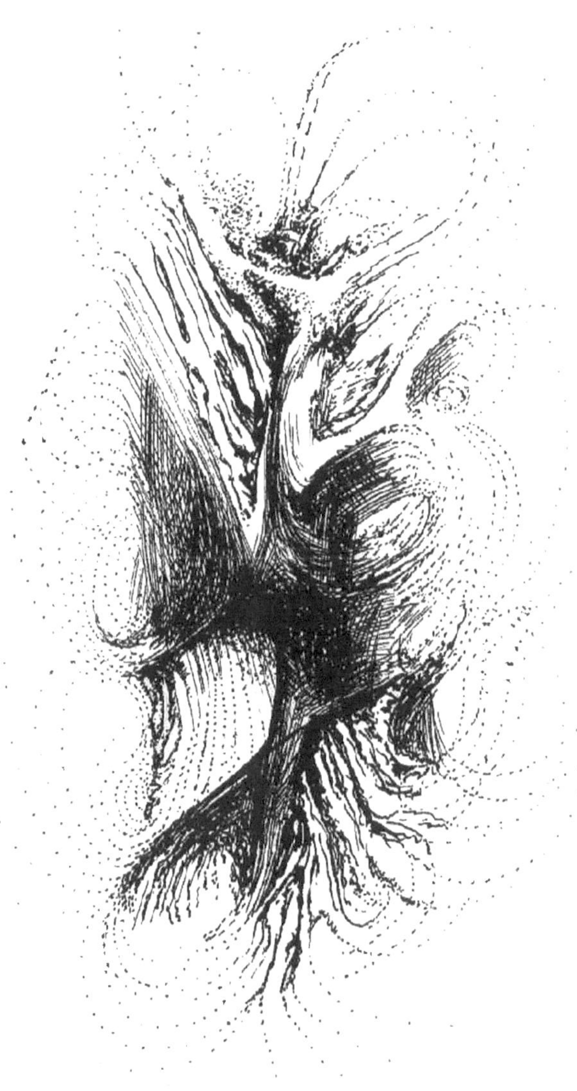

Eric Basso. *Untitled.* 1978

ERIC BASSO. *Untitled.* 1977.

ERIC BASSO

Malovealis
a paradox pecks at the widow's ear
it climbs into bed beside her
the beer has done its work
winter is coming on now
nights long enough to sustain
rumors of the madness in each house

the horse tumbles off the roof
is caught by a butterfly net
before its hooves can scatter sparks
across the shattered paving stones
it sniffs the scent of the woman
who's just turned the corner

who moves under the widow's window
toward a sound only she can hear
the whisper of a scarred hand
brushing against a table leg
she'd like to go inside but hasn't
been invited anywhere for years

her father's name was Malovealis
a river ran through a mill town
called Malovealis you can
still find it on the map if you use
a really powerful microscope
but this has nothing to do with that

or with the man warming his hands
over that smoking rubbish heap
he hopes to see a fire in the sky

and though it will never happen
fire becomes the bone of a memory
Lodged at the back of his throat

the chintz curtains and the chair
where the mice were singing
years from now they will be
the subject of an old photograph
a blip on the back of the monster
Between this eternity and the next

December 10, 1993

STILL LIFE WITH WINTER

hands that would be stilled
by the bright flame of noon
are buried in the bedrock
of an extinct planet
at the foot of the yard

Malovealis walked out one night
into the dead of it and became
the fly in a lump of amber
he never returned to the house
where his daughter was waiting

ice husks the trees
the heaviest boot leaves
no impression in the snow
from my window I can smell
the blue of the cold

January 21, 1994

In Memoriam

Dob Kamperelic
1947-2020
International Mailartist
Publisher of Open World
With thanks

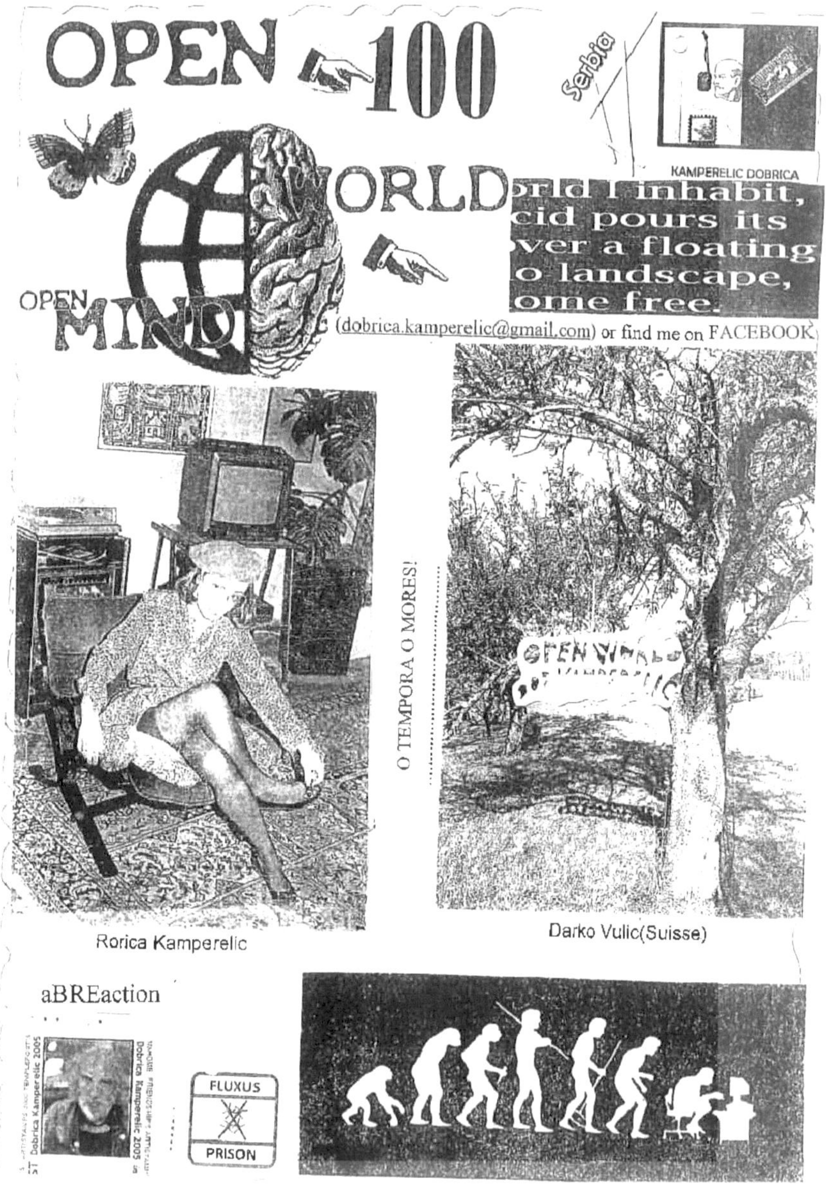

OPEN 100

OPEN MIND WORLD

Serbia

KAMPERELIC DOBRICA

...rld I inhabit,
...cid pours its
...ver a floating
...o landscape,
...ome free.

(dobrica.kamperelic@gmail.com) or find me on FACEBOOK

O TEMPORA O MORES!

Rorica Kamperelic

Darko Vulic(Suisse)

aBREaction

Artist, Provocateur*

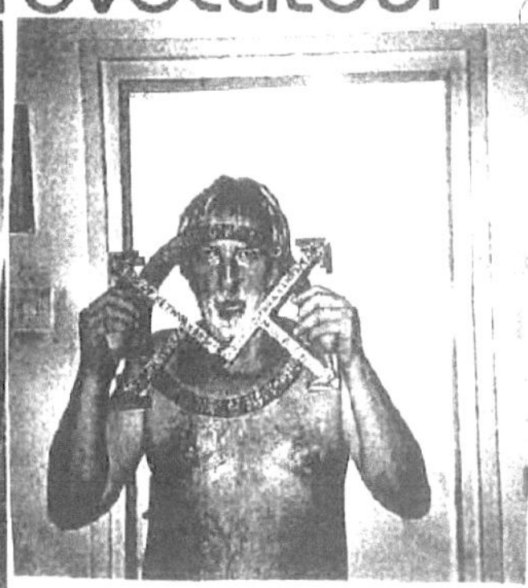

c/o Rorica & Dob Kamperelić.
Ustanička 152/73 Belgrade, Serbija

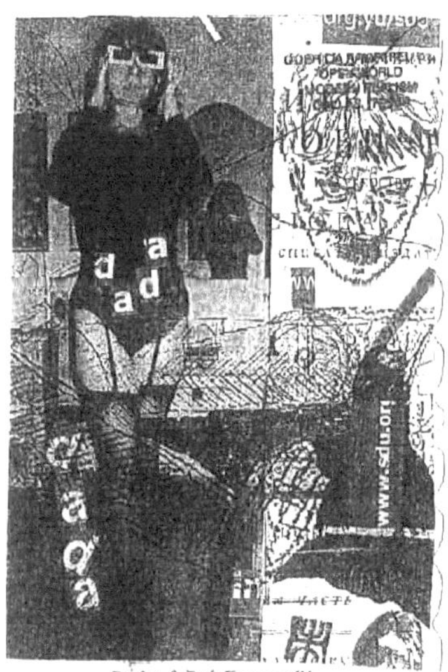

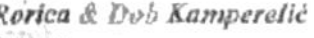

Rorica & Dob Kamperelić

Rorica & Dob Kampereli

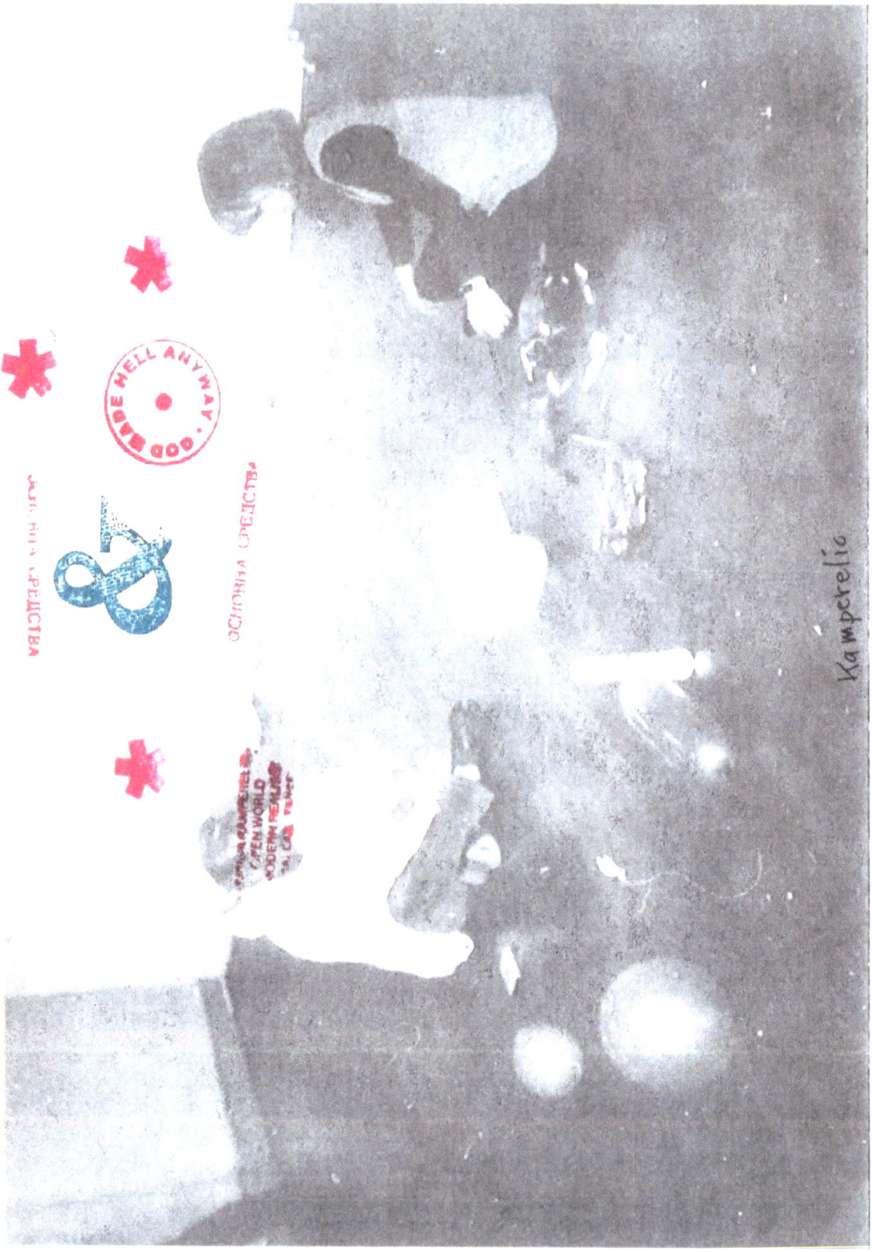
GOD MADE HELL ANYWAY
Kamperelia

I scream

into

the **endless void**

of your unlived life

a rain bird

born without wings

Jessica.
2/2/1989 – 11/2/2019

I will love you forever.

Vultures by Darlene Altschul June 2015

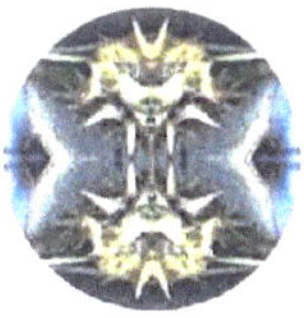

SKIES OPEN sleep upright and watch the gate TORN SPARKLE eight route ways and a long smile h

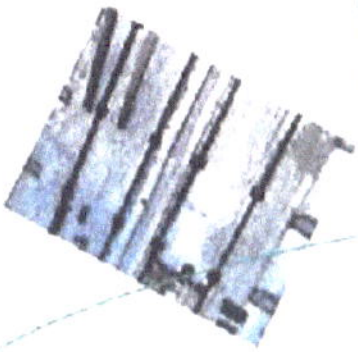

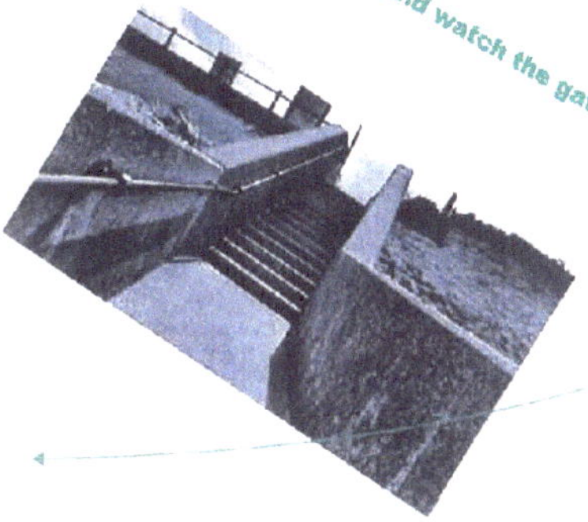

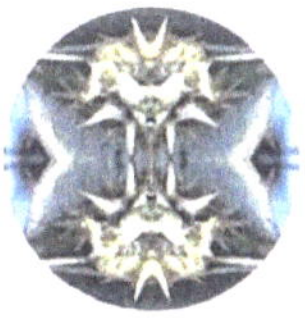

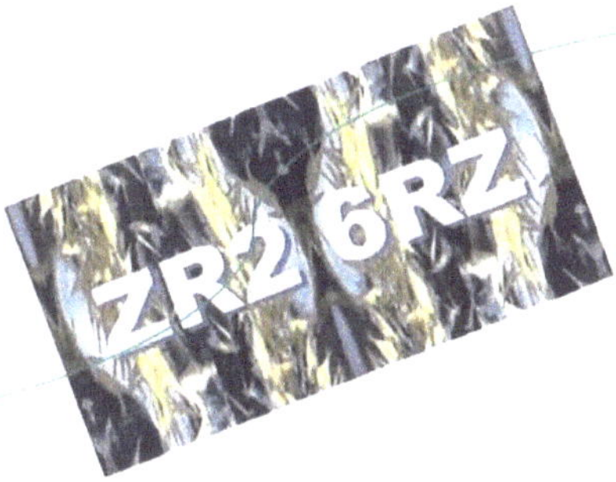

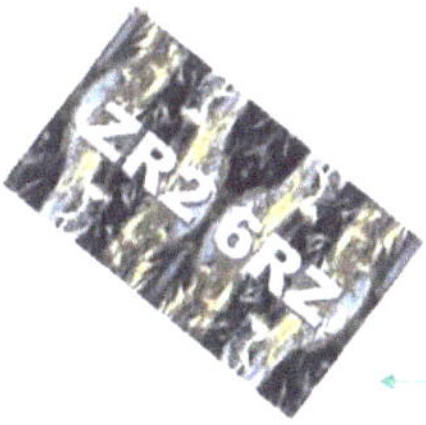

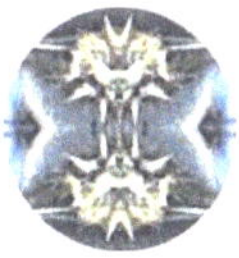

Alwina

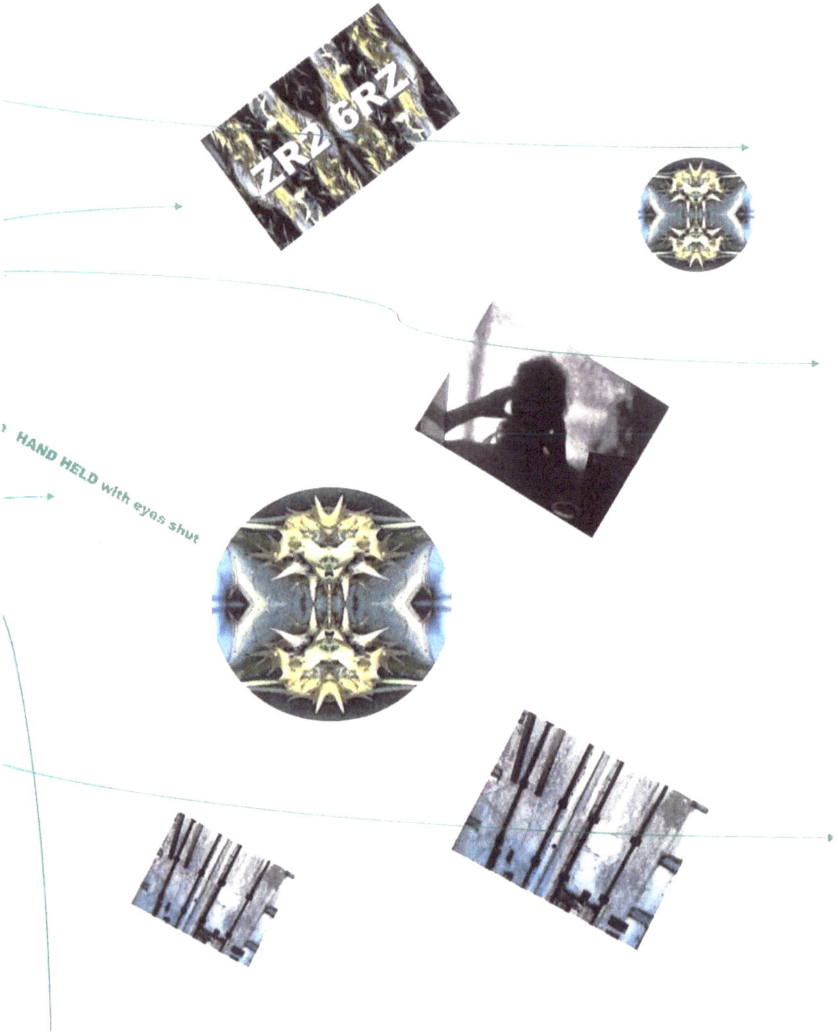

ZR2 6RZ

HAND HELD with eyes shut

NORTH PULLS

the southern SPARK ZONE to stretch a groove within the ice

Alwina

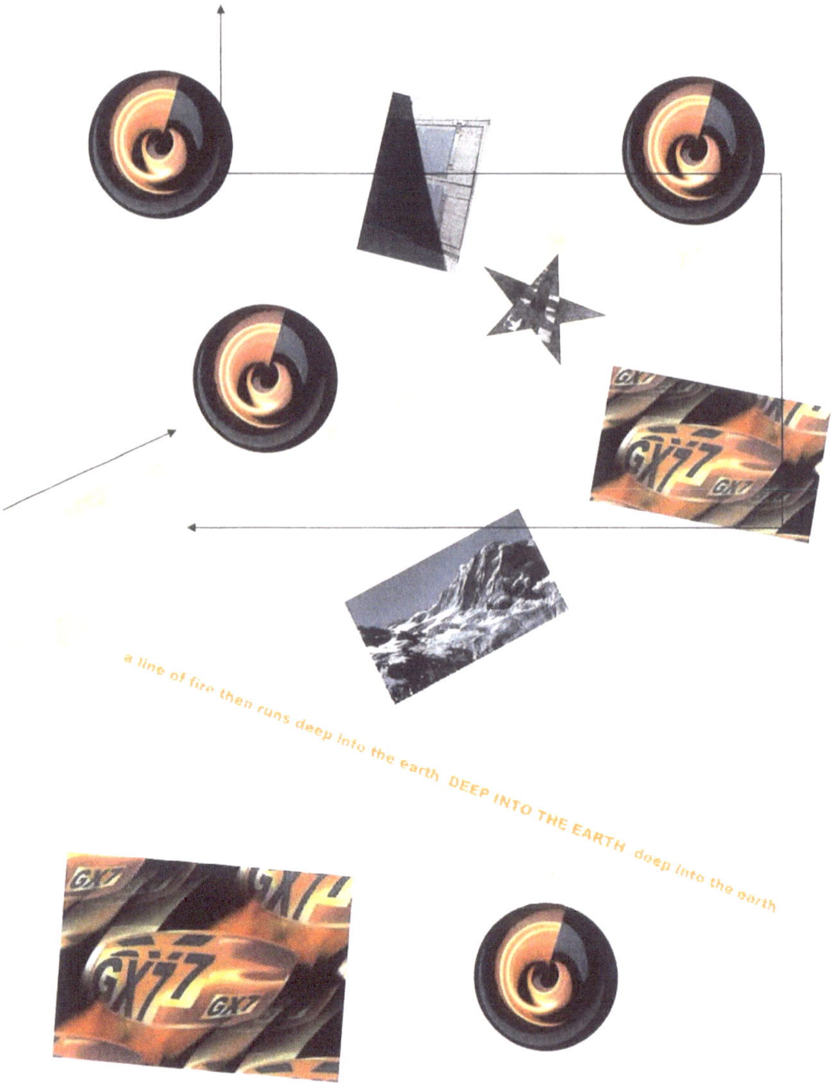

a line of fire then runs deep into the earth DEEP INTO THE EARTH deep into the earth

Aponte

Threshold

Inner most light
when unleashed
joy of the star
stardust alive
us we are
floating through
void of space
a joyful dance
all memories unleashed
unified with all
with no path estranged
love guides shinning

David Stanley Aponte
15.January.2003

Michael S. Begnal

Féin Eile

On the old cow-road
from hotel to old hotel,
from dirty restaurant to lunch counter,
to reach a soiled room
Sroichim seomra seargtha
ina bhfuil beirt elle,
two others—
a punk artist
from the 80s hardcore scene
making paintings,
ag taistil leis an ngiotáraí
ón mbanna ceoil Agnostic Front,
And now in this dirty room
worried and upset as I am

muid ag caint
and the artist intimates
that he was raised through the medium
of Irish, even though he, his family
were from the city of New York
                        Nua Eabhrac-

   "Tá sé sin iontach," I reply
le glór grágach, "comhghairdeas"
(in caw-like voice),
"an bhfuil sí fós agat?"
                  and this brought tears out of his eyes,
                  and I was sorry, already sorrowful,
                  told him I was sorry,
                        As Béarla

Michael S. Begnal

Palindrome IX

Easily identified
as a torture truck,
aluminum sides, paneling
in which framed small squares
of pink skin,
soft and warm and crushed
in the next lane,
and driving the cab:
someone who should consider
    suicide

    six-eyed
somnambulist gone,
intervention came
in the neck, line,
shaft in, swarmed in, scorched
off pink skin
sandwiched, farmed, small squares
aluminum, shades pummeling,
as a door, tar-dark
as a lie, a tender foot

Michael S. Begnal

Flying

1.

The river muddy and brown,
swollen after recent rain

      two birds aflight
      flying toward
      he vanishing point of
         sun arise above
             [no dream, instead
             lighton limitless walls]

2.

two bats
cavorting
spinning
out from the cave jag
in humid night
cutting into the air,

black above
blue horizon   [iron-blue]
—the illusory line—
between earth and ether
     cuts
the human head [head a vast black]

3.
hummingbird
   hovers smiling,   [the edge of the beak]
the river moving over rock,

   electric wires
plunge down from the cliff
above the far bank,
and back-woods confederate flags/   [Polaroids of rubbery dead]
two hummingbirds
   hover off the balcony

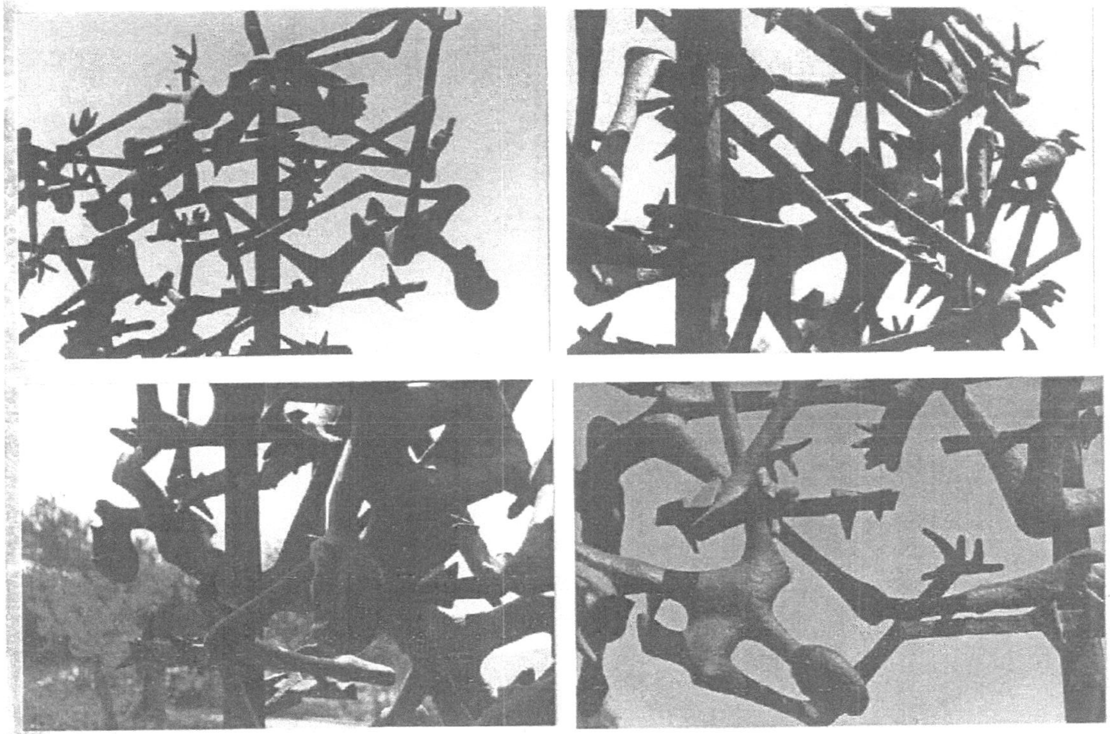

Yad Vashem

Burrus

Either Or

After the event I saw a series of sketches,
figures who define themselves by Giacometti ambiguity.

Conversation drips into French New Wave.
Jean-Luc backlit a frame of collapsed zinnias
that border our Hackensack wood planked walkway
all the way from the house to the Studebaker,
where in collective silence a swarm of ladybugs
foxtrot to polka dots wrapped in trembling shadows.

Two houses down finalist lick their wounds.
In the aftershock, even when splicing looks end to end
no one is handsome before dawn.
We lose ourselves in order to find ourselves.

I'm still lost.

Burrus

Expedition South of Tunis
(El Jem to be exact)

They consider me a catalog.
My name is smeared across mirrors.
Nothing is taped to the walls or visible
      through Chartres stained glass,
I'm worn like South Sea pearls.
I should be outlawed- verboten.

My mother had many *Simplicity* patterns.
She didn't need them.
I remember all the shirts she made on the *Singer.*
I considered them designer boutique.

Here the afternoon light sleeps
      under a baroque gauze. I chase it.
Chatter prompts more questions, forgotten moments
salute Klee and take shattered Bardo mosaics
to a parking garage where they're read like tea leaves
and given two coats of rapid dry paint- cerulean blue.

My past is not revealed.

Burrus

A Curl of Fog Cloaks Grieving Odalisques

They fly around us like enflamed guitar strings
playing a Nat King Cole impromptu.
Our breath dances across the Grand Erg Oriental,
a bagpipe chorus hums support- admission's gratis.

I will be your guide and show you where you've been.
Places you've forgotten.
You swim faster against the current (a real surprise)
until the foam burns to doubt,
       tasting of campfire s'mores.

You sputter around the coals like a balloon releasing air.
The absinthe filling your eyes makes us wet
       under a scorpion purple sky.
Crossing the center line your two lane expressions blur.
We're on a highway of lost calculations-
no scenic turnouts, only wind chimes swaying
to candle flames in sync with Pachelbel.

We've smelled this sunset before.
I'll store your promise in a tortoise shell box,
next to black licorice, an emerald, Milk Duds,
       and my high school ring.

I may include our photo booth shots.

Burrus

A Labyrinth of False Starts

I remember when the red bandana flagman would wave
as he clanged passed the crossing gate.
Our train's late. More than an hour.
We walk across thick dust for a cold drink.
She asks for specific details about our destination
      as if I have a map.
The bartender checks his watch, nods,
and points south, giving me hope.

The broken pieces beneath our feet
she claims are from Carthage. Or maybe Sardinia.
She picks up a tiny mosaic depicting a geometric pattern
And hands it to me. A show of trust she says.
I expected to see statues, at least an aqueduct.

The sun feels much hotter. She removes a cap
from her shoulder bag and puts it on.
"Can we have another beer?"
I signal the waiter.

She squints as she looks up at the pale blue sky. "
Can we count stars even if we can't see them?"
"Where did you hear that?"
"From a lobster fisherman."

The train's whistle cuts through the dry, soft air.
I put money on the table and pick up our bags.
"I can see three stars...no, five."

BURRUS

Many kinds of fish
Rig activity
Colt AR-15 (U.S.)
• About 400,000 manufactured; cannot be reimported.
• Comes with a five-round detachable box magazine; usually fitted with a 30-round magazine, with capacity for more.
WORLD'S HIGHEST STANDARD OF LIVI
There's no wa
like the
American Way
A
B
C

Continuum
Burrus

Catlin

Ice storm
arrives
with night

train sounds,
directions,
changing

with the wind

First from Northeast
then the Southwest,
all swirling,
Becoming as one

Becoming
a gyre,
a confusion

of failed
noise

and light

wind hollowing
crevices
for the unspeakable

dead to be
resurrected
in accordance

with plans passenger
Train schedules

the forlorn warning
whistles herald
the beginning
of graveyard shifts

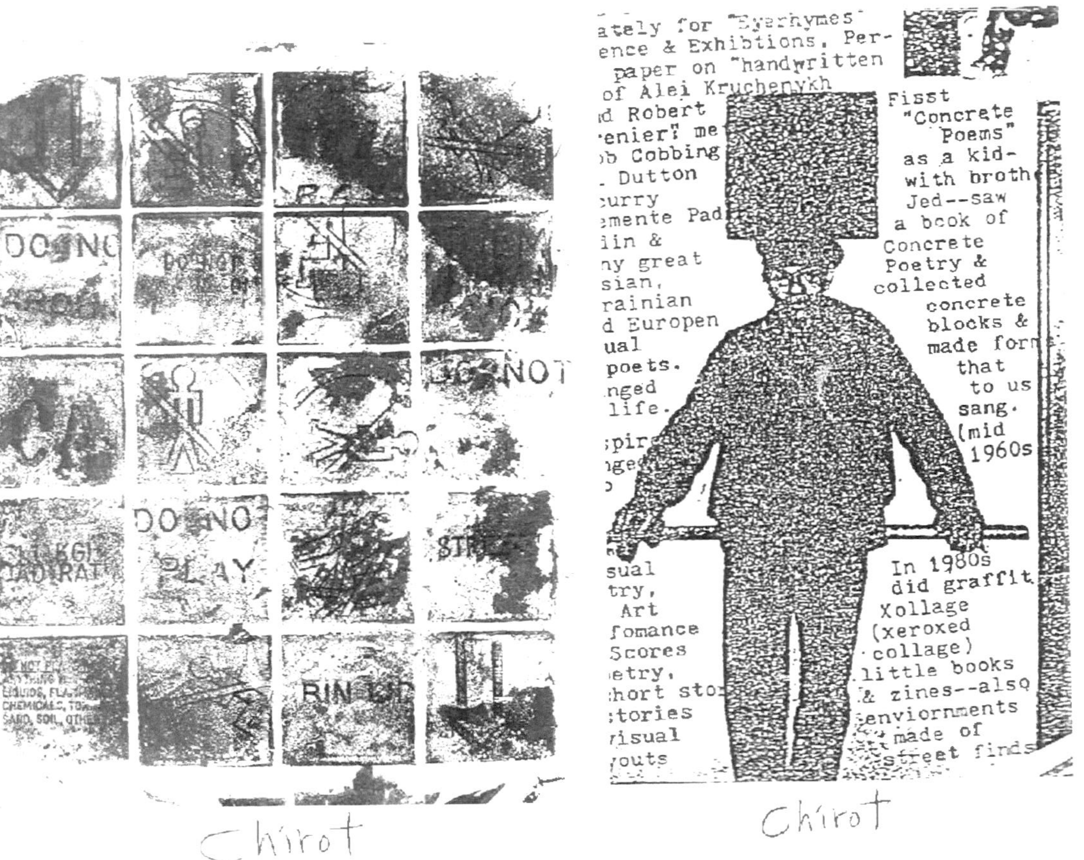

ately for "Eyerhymes"
ence & Exhibitions. Per-
paper on "handwritten
of Alei Kruchenykh
d Robert
enier? me
b Cobbing
. Dutton
urry
emente Pad
lin &
ny great
sian,
rainian
d Europen
ual
poets.
nged
life.
spir
nge
Fisst
"Concrete
Poems"
as a kid-
with broth
Jed--saw
a book of
Concrete
Poetry &
collected
concrete
blocks &
made form
that
to us
sang.
(mid
1960s
sual
try,
Art
fomance
Scores
etry,
hort sto
tories
visual
youts
In 1980s
did graffit
Xollage
(xeroxed
collage)
little books
& zines--also
enviorments
made of
street finds
DO NO
DO NOT
CA
LARGE
ADVRAT
DO NO
PLAY
STR
RIN UP
DO NOT
Chirot
Chirot

high above
the wall...
the 1-winged
Blackbird
the Poem
Chirot

INTERNATIONAL CONFERENCE ON

THE LESSONS OF THE HOLOCAUST

The Living Witness
Art in the Concentration Camps

UNDER THE AUSPICES OF THE
COORDINATING COUNCIL ON THE HOLOCAUST
MEMORIAL COMMITTEE FOR THE SIX MILLION JEWISH MARTYRS
NATIONAL INSTITUTE ON THE HOLOCAUST

MUSEUM OF AMERICAN JEWISH HISTORY
55 North Fifth Street, Philadelphia, Pennsylvania

October 18 - November 19, 1978

DRAWING MADE FROM A FOUND
DRAWING
MIKE DYAR   2018

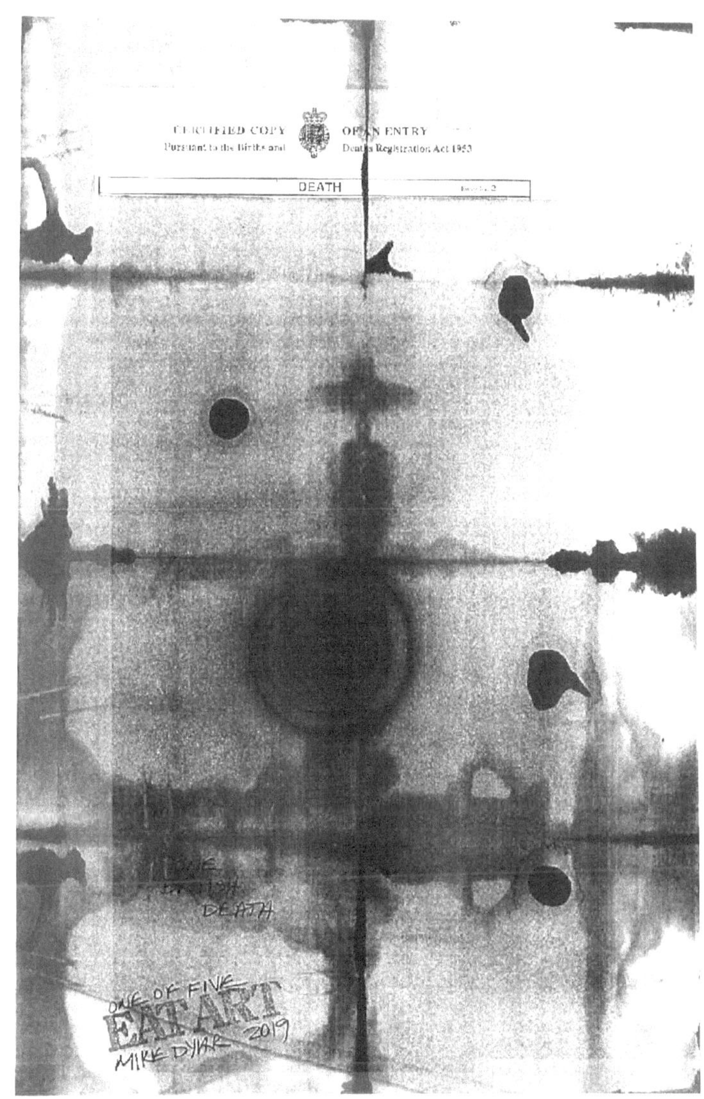
CERTIFIED COPY OF AN ENTRY
Pursuant to the Births and Deaths Registration Act 1953
DEATH
DEATH
ONE OF FIVE
EAT ART
MIKE DYBR 2019

McArthur Gunter

A COSMIC SUN: AN ASTRONOMICAL, SPATIAL AND MULTIDIMENSIONAL PORTRAIT OF A CHINESE REVOLUTIONARY (SUN YAT-SEN)

1

Sublimely
Stirred by the magnificent zenith of the marvelous
Sunrise
Sagas of the Taiping Rebels dazzling and
Subversive aurora borealis display and in the romantic
Spirit of legendary monster-slayers of ancient epochs,
Sun Yat-sen was that providential Chung kuo "Morning
Star," a chosen heavenly
Son born on the twelfth day of the
Sterling eleventh month of the "Moon of Falling Leaves"
Simultaneously the three hundredth and
Sixteenth day and the forty
Sixth 'Monday in the Year of the
Siberian tiger in the
Sixty
Sixth year of the nineteenth century in
Synchronous timing with the
Steadfast celestial Leonid meteor
Showers from the eighteen hundred and
Sixty
Sixth Comet One.
Sun was the blessed
Son for the revolutionary
Second Coming of a New Golden Cultural Age

Surpassing the glorious resurrection of the
Stunning Tang New Morning to the
Swinging and foot
Stomping
Syncopation of "Down
South Camp Meeting"!

2

Spatially and
Surrealistically dreaming and
Spacetraveling elliptically through the Zodiac at
Supersonic
Speed from interstellar
Space through time warps from the Fifth Dimension
Sun
Surveyed the geopolitical landscape from the
Stratosphere like a mystic
Seer with telescopic divination equipped with
Special geometrically
Shaped Kuomintang reflecting and refracting lenses in the
Strategic Tour Directions and all
Seminal cardinal points in between. He
Startlingly witnessed the multidimensional cataclysms of
Social firestorms, political earthquakes, economic
Sand dunes, military tornadoes, imperial
Stone
Showers; moral fogs, ethical dust
Storms, philosophical quicksands, alien principles and
Spiritual maelstroms; monsoons of graft which
Stymied the people with
Scarlet hearts, patriotic ghosts, religious mirages,
Sporadic oases of courage;
Skeptical prophecies, holy apparitions, dissociated
States, punctured pride, immolated deeds, tortured

Solace, flammable families, lacerated love;
Slaughtered
Silhouetted
Sacts, anemic happiness, anxious prophecies, nether
Seances, bleeding minds, pilloried peace, psychological
Sunspots, crucified
Simpleness,
Suicidal
Spirits;
Slim
Secessions, radical visions, revolutionary daydreams;
Sinister
Sellouts, hijacked Hong Kong held hostage,
Slit nobleness, neurotic dynasties, decapitated demonstrations,
Strangled
Sermons, manic manifestos, rash reasoning,
Strangely feverish delicacies, raped innocence,
Scapegoated
Scrolls, hysterical fortitude, delusory discipline;
Shackled
Sages, phobic duty, melancholic dialogues,
Somnambulistic
Scholars, mangled metaphysics, mythic nightmares;
Skidding
Shamefulness, terrorized honesty, hallucinatory dignity,
Selfish
Scoundrels, pestilenced prudence, quartered merit,
Sabotaged justice, ruptured rights, gorged goodness,
Shanghaied freedom, foreign financial locusts, fragile
Sleep patterns; and
Screaming
Souls in deep gorges and rift valleys and on high mountain
Steppes and cliffs and innumerably lucid
Saffron bodies

Shaped like white lotus plants and
Straw-hued lakes with bloated and floating brains
Shaped like yellowish red poppies and other bodies and brains
Simulating tranced
States with the bodies exhaling and inhaling in cycles of
Seven out-of-body experiences in opium
Streams in an overall general, cultural
Shock of gas and dust resembling the turbulent
Solar remnant of a Crab Nebula or like the
Supervening impact from the
Serial bombardment of giant asteroids from the
Senior Oort Asteroid Belt to the
Solemn
Syncopation of "Chimes Blues".

3

Sun's cum laude trust, magnum cum laude faith and
Summa cum laude love as mediums
Surged in a
Sapphire heart
Surrounded by a
Shimmering chrome-yellow corona; and like a neutron
Star pulsated electromagnetic wave messages of
Socialism as naturally nutritious as brown rice
Supported by Nationalism as indigenous as the
Stately giant panda and Democracy as
Salutatory and bountiful as the Yellow
Sea; and he promised to personally deliver those goods
Special delivery to the powerfully earthy and
Syncopated cornet rhythm of "Oriental
Strut"!

4

Silky

Smooth with the phantom-like weaves of a dynamic
Shooting
Star,
Sun, by a
Split
Second,
Successfully dodged the colossal Qing Asteroid
Swung wildly and
Slyly from the outer limits of the
Stratosphere which originated from the
Space
Satellite
Station in the Union Jack
Solar
System during the "Moon of Changing
Seasons".
Sun presciently perceived it as a
Serene omen for his revolutionary coterie and
Service and Cosmic destiny like an entranced
Son endowed with a
Sophisticated
Sixth
Sense to the honey-combed cornet
Syncopation of the marvelously beautiful and hypnotic
"Sweet Like This".

scoobidoobidoo
between the Big Bang & the Big Crunch
& all the Theories Of Everything
the pillar-models of what should sustain
the grammar of fatality

HUMANS

earthborne mortals, reasonable fellowmen
those who permit & intervene
the anthro- & the holocene
post-once-upon-ity of stock-exchanges
past perfect, present perfect, future perfect
consumer of this one & common Planet
ruiner of seed & progeny
ahead of time
green utopia, yes
we try again next friday
scoobidoobidoo

nula horo
wolfgang günther
kassel, germany
(w.guenther.esperanto@web.de)
2019

Open final
(parapantoun 111)

the range of sudden & the elements of vicnity
scoop sea in transit & going dry to follow
saving seeds & then again a specious argument
spot more now & just even can do

scoop sea in transit & going dry to follow
motherly lots of fire & so adverse whats-&-wants
spot more now & just even can do
where humans are, a sokrates & forward to

motherly lots of fire & so adversive whats-&-wants
off homo zappiens & the fact of lotteries
where humans are, a sokrates & forward to
a metaphoric sun & brotherly compassion

off homo zappiens & the fact of lotteries
saving seeds & then again a specious argument
a metaphoric sun & brotherly compassion
the range of sudden & the elements of vicinity
nula horo
(from the esperanto)
wolfgang gunther
(w.guenther.esperanto@web.de)
kassel, germany
2019

Posology of sounds
(Parapantoun)

Loving all the random music playing viruses...
I'm sorry to absquatulate the Hall of Bardolatry.
The ruckus of the hooligans as final cause of phonophobia.
A fipple underwent unnoticed cacoethes.

I'm sorry to absquatulate the Hall of Bardolatry.
Imperious debauchery with highpitched giggle.
A fipple underwent unnoticed cacoethes.
As I just said: No hemidemisemiquavers after midnight.

Imperious debauchery with highpitched giggle.
Listen: Gardyloo! and Mazel tov!
As I just said: No hemidemisemiquavers after midnight.
Discombobulation of brouhahas and compulsive the eructations.

Listen: Gardyloo! and Mazel tov!
The ruckus of the hooligans as final cause of phonophobia.
Discombobulation of brouhahas and compulsive the eructations.
Loving all the random music playing viruses...

Nula Horo
Wolfgang Gunther,
Kassel, Germany
(W.gunther.espranto@web.de)
2018

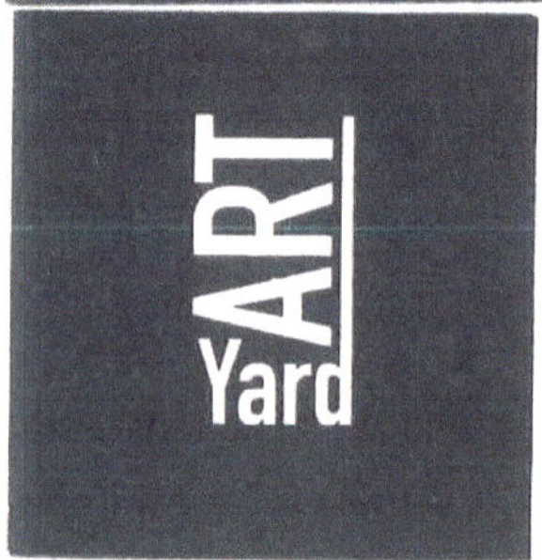

ARTYARD
62A Trenton Ave
Frenchtown, NJ
08825

GALLERY HOURS
Wednesday through Sunday
11:00 AM - 5:00 PM

www.artyard.org
contact@artyard.org
Instagram: @artyardcenter
Facebook.com/artyardfrenchtown

Found
Faith Heisler

Be like a **bird**, who, halting in her flight

On a limb too slight, feels it give way beneath her;

Yet sings, sings, knowing she has wings;

Yet sings, sings, knowing she has wings.

--based on a quote by Victor Hugo

Heisler

BLACKBIRD IN EUCLIDEAN SPACE

CHECKING THE MAILBOX

JANKE

Der Karotten Kaese Kuchen ist aber Riessengrass..
    Genoss. Er schmeckt aber sehr gut.
Na ja freilich, teilt er sich selber aus..
unseretwegegen.. (Aufstehen. Austeilen.
Sofort!) Aber Schmeckts!
Diese Gedicht scheint mir als nicht Komplett.
Ohne Genugtuung. Wohin Denn? Welche Richtung?

Looky Here, Mighty Big NYC
ails want from you
is more respect, more
appreciation, more
nourishment...
No, Heidi, I don't want
another of your world-
ly displays of affection,
(PDAs) I'd rather have a
dreamy walk sequence on
Lindnerstrasse, or, better
yet, a quick creep downstairs
to our secret lovenests
Why Schatz, you've already
stowed our shoes in the
little cubby -- how sweet!
And your shoes, why they're
amazing, in need of praising,
all jewelled up! (The East
German Moose is loose!)
The red bricks explode upwards!
Wait! What do I hear? Why
it's the Werner von Braun Eye
-Brow Radio Funk Orchestra!
They're all fired up" "My be-
loved listeners" etc.

The carrot cheese cake is huge
my friend. It tastes great!
Just for us, it's divvying it
self up & delivering the goods.
Yum!
This poem somehow feels incom
plete. Unsatisfying. Where
to go with it?)

R. Kimm

Origins: I wish to thank Mark Sonnenfeld for his excellent poem <u>Look NYC.</u> I wrote the fon̄owing version in <u>Homage</u> style, first in German, then translating it "back" into English. Sept. 2019.

       Schau Mal Her du Gross-Stadt NYC

       Mir: mehr geniessen, vergnuegen, spass
machen, nit vergessen, unter-stutz-en (ach ja "nuchtern"
       soll'sedenn heissen.)
Ich will nit "stossen" mir Dir Heidi im Aussen-Draussen,
       rund & rum .. aber im Gegenteil schon mal wirklich
       schoen spazieren gehen under den Linden (traeumlicherweise)
       (oder, lieber)
       schon wiedermal under den Treppen
       demnaechst in unseren. Keller
       Liebesnest kriechen:
       Kuch-a-mal Schatz, wie frueher,
       hast du schon unsere Schuen
       schoen weg-gesteckt (deinen sind
       beschmoocht, glaenzend) Ach ja
       die beschmoochten schooen sind
       wieder los auf der Stroos!
(und) Die Roten Ziegel springen in die Luft...
Moment mal ich hoere schon wieder das Weltberuhmten
       Werner von Braun Augenbrauen Radio Funk
       Orkestra.. "Meinen beliebten Zuhoerer"
       Und platscht's los!

Solamito

MAIL ART

Solarito

BLACKBIRD

10 APR 2018

BLACKBIRD
Sobarto

64

BLACKBIRD

Solanto

BLACK BIRD
Solantto

Solanito

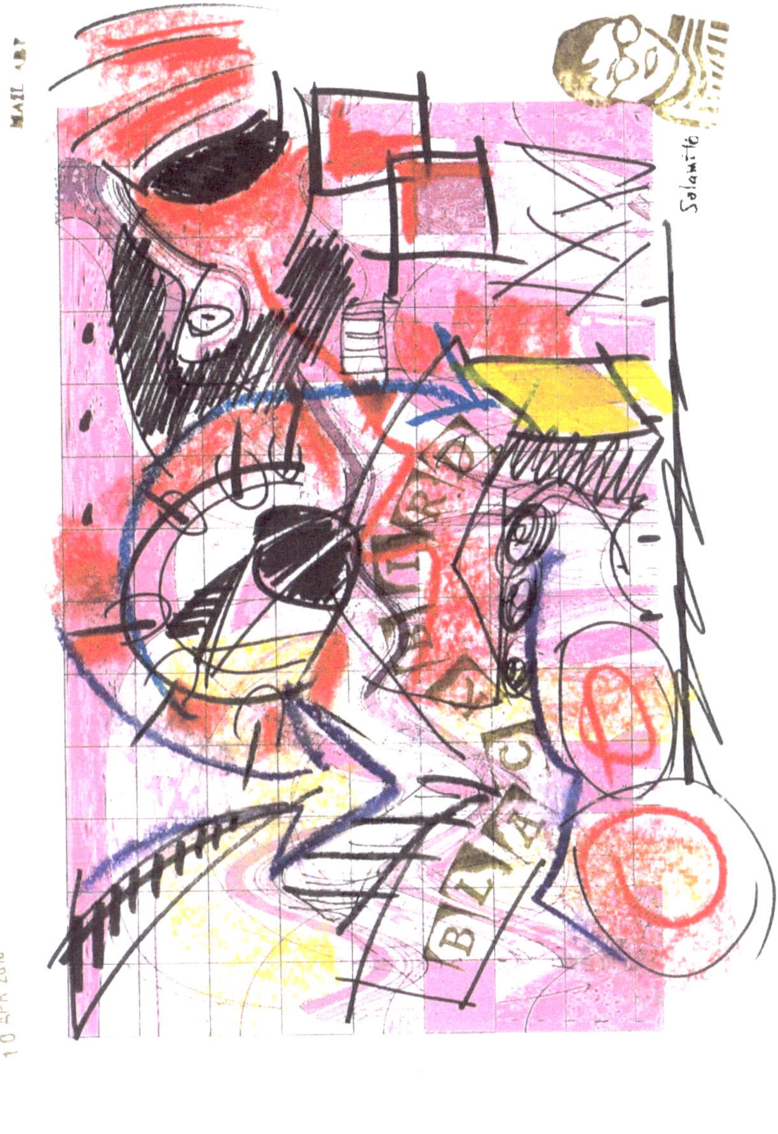
MAIL ART
10 APR 2018
BLACK
Solamito

MAIL ART
BLACKBIRD
Solamito
16 ABR 2018

McNamara

237
I META-NETWORKER IN SPIRIT
RUGGERO MAGGI
allarg.
_mor!
Oh! Al_fredo, il crudo termine ser_bato al nostro amor!
m'uccic
io do_lor, m'uc_
a tempo
_ide il tuo d
an_tol_mo_
POST ART
RUGGERO MAGGI
ri_o la
tta mi al
G

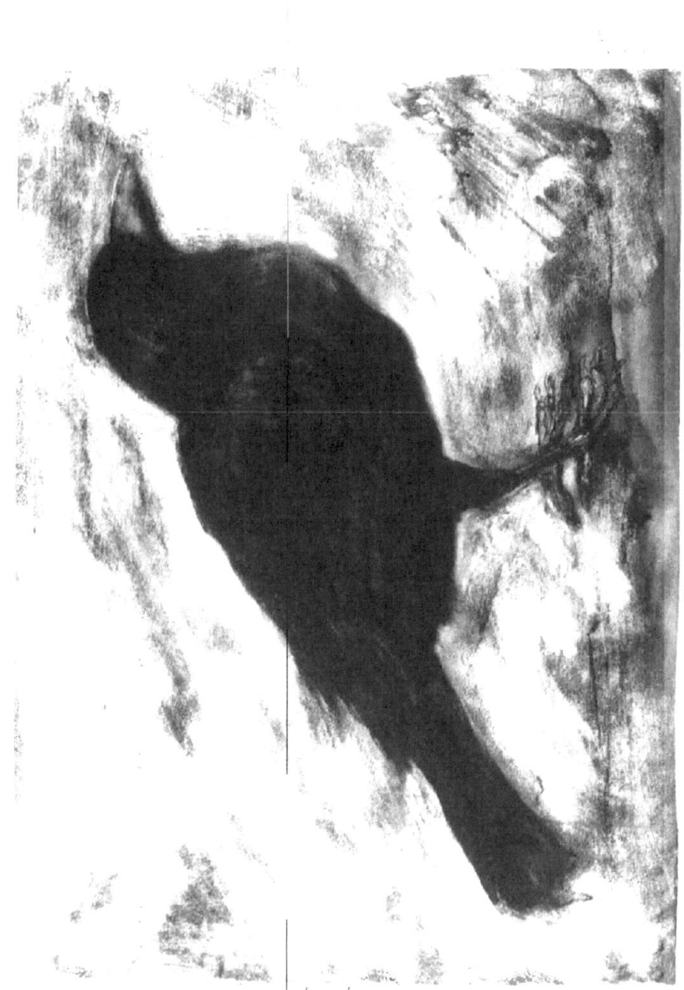

Mailarta

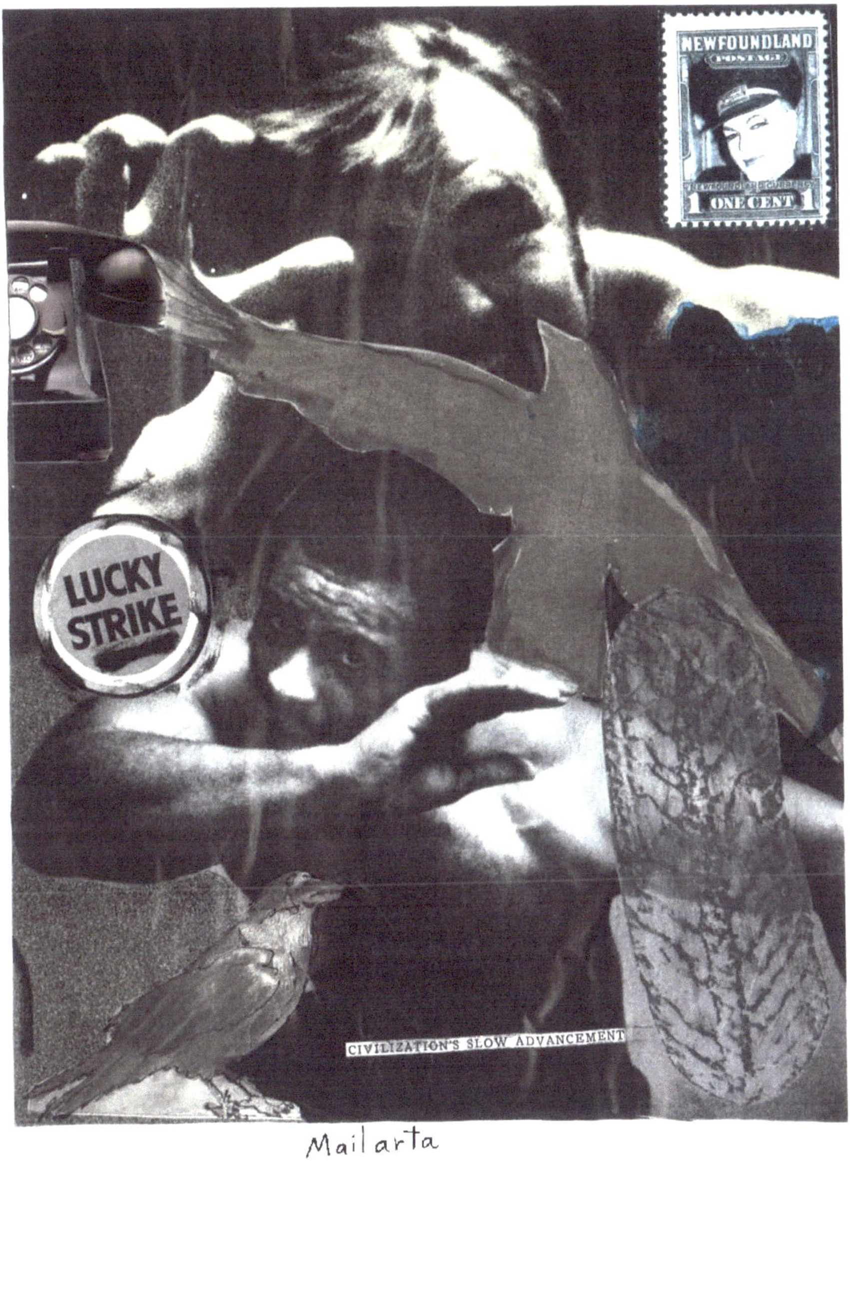
NEWFOUNDLAND
POSTAGE
1 ONE CENT 1
LUCKY
STRIKE
CIVILIZATION'S SLOW ADVANCEMENT

Mailarta

DEKLARACIJA ZA KOVERAT
naziv i tip koverte: TIP D
dimenzija koverte:
    - spoljašnja: 200 x 275 mm
    - unutrašnja: 180 x 265 mm
proizvođač: VP Group
zamlja porekla: Nemačka
uvoznik koverte: Beoteleprom,
Kumodraška 257, Beograd, tel: 2466-131
datum proizvodnje/godina uvoza: 2016.

Макс Ернст, Без наслова, 1923.

Collaboration: Carolyn Cline - blackbird paper cut-out
Katerina Nikoltsou - marble-color paint

Nikoltsou

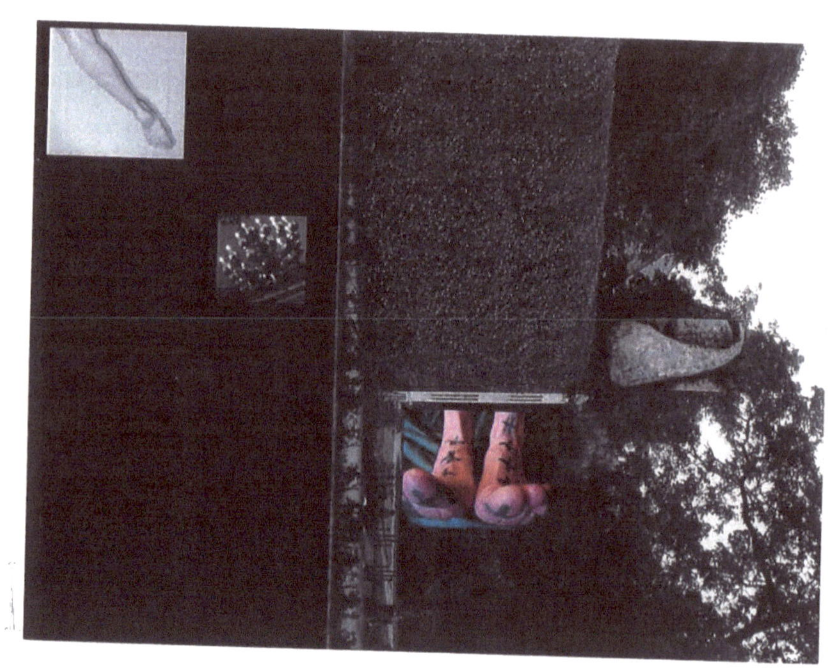

NISS

"I speak for none of your kind
I speak for the end of the owls"

-- Hans Magnus Enzenberger --

Ghostsong For The Masses

Rain sun,sun rain
&so it is raining today & I oil my old feet
As the broken shadows of the Parthenon fall upon the hills of
The Acropolous falling upon the little vendors table in the
Market stalls of The Plaka where lay tiny statues of dead gods &
New racing forms
As aging Corinthian lemons disintegrate into dispirate dust.

Who will predict the Messiah's arrival?
Genesis to Job to Isaiah
Rain falls on the olives in the Garden of Gethsemane
The Final Hour approaches: on shadowed wind feet
Morning comes & the sky is filled with men whose wings are
Too small to fly & so
The End of Days, like finally A human eraser,
Erasing all lines once drawn in the sand & so
Rain sun, sun rain
The End of Days
I taste my sobs.

&it is raining today
Donatello's skidrow Magdalene is weeping &
The Northern Lights are colored black & white &
The Ruins are speaking well-practiced lines from the Bible &
The Koran &
The Bhagavad Gita
Scaring alleycats from the alley &
Lantern fish from the sea.

&it is raining today in Damascus

In the slums of Ramala
In the Valley of Lepers
Beneath the lip of the Los Angeles Loop
Raining today upon Blake's angel-filled trees
Cupid in a rain coat becomes a bitter boy &
In the Kremlin, Pyongyang & Trump Tower silver Whips
Are cracking &
A reckoning rain from a halocaust sky is falling
Upon the slavegirl faces of Boko Haram
Black rain falling on bumpstock parades
Children de-sensitized into adults
Adults industrialized into cancerous bone.

In the same way
Hurricane Sandy is eaten by Hurricane Katrina
Is eaten by Harvey &
Irma Ave Maria &
Super-Typhoon Megi
Is eaten by UberaSuperTyphoon Huiyan

2 - - - Ghostsong <u>for The Masses</u>
In the same way
Emperor Franz Joseph's Joyful Apocalypse is approaching
In the same way
When the doves come out, the hunters are armed
In the same way
Master Dada high steps from the Scripture of the storm
Wearing a fine well-tailored suit.
Hens cackling at dawn
Lord Hawk makes his rounds
John Muir at the foot of the Holy Mountain quietly
Rehearses his Ghostsong for the Masses
Rain sun, sun rain

On the roof the bluesman is tapping
Tap   Tap   Tap   to the beat
Of bonzai traffic & Cossack horses.
& so, I oil my old feet

My olfactories well greased with the fragrance of the gilly flower
Which give way to the sweet breath of the passion flower
Which bow to the nosegays & jasmine.

July/2018

Normal

Babel
Where the
Babble
Began
Cheryl Penn
Edition 2
·BABEL ON·
GENESIS · 11

make us a name

BBaabbbbl
Babblreeeeeeb
BBaabbbbllle
BBaabbbbl
BBBABBBLLLEEE
Babble
Babble
Babel
Confusion
Did you know that?
whhhherrrBablbbeellleeellll
BBaabbbbl
BBBABBBLLLEEE
Babble

Cross words unknown words Babble
Babel where the Babble began Babel

He made R430
n the
Bbbbobbblllleeeeeaaanab
Bbbbaaaa
Bbbbbaa
Bbbbbaa
2018

THE UNFINISHED BOOK

By Cheryl Penn

Don't make excuses,
don't tell lies
the TRUTH WILL ALWAYS OUT -
all dressed up with nowhere to go
except picnic lunches and dangerous schemes-
swallows and seagulls
on every page.
Anonymous signals
awful interruptions-
the suspense was terrible
too horrible
because
SOMETHING was about to happen.

1
Dice roll

ink spills

did he think
he would get away with it?

darkness seeps
twilight sinks
heaviness takes its toll.
magic cars in rearview mirrors,
life on hold
while bridges burn at dusk
with 45 minutes to go

2
water ripples
reflections of faces gone
neon replications,
her hair, falling across her face
remembering forbidden - unbidden love.
Fir trees
more ink spills
but no one was drawing.

shifting sand in hour glasses
forest hideouts
with foreign cars parked in front
and trees
always leaning inwards - **darkly**
a nightmare I cant wake up from.

3
Things happened
without my meaning them to
small things
strange things
all adding up
to a disaster doused with oil
a fire
which set the world alight
my world.

4
a broad smile
angelic voices
in green walls
should he/shouldn't he?
he did and it was all a rush.
guitar strums and wise men said

when the spotlight falls, **RUN!**
Innocence fell as the curtain falls
and driftwood becomes our home.

5
tired of the solitude,
so very tired,
she broke my heart -
so brave - **the mirror of my mind..**

6
it's easier to write about the world
than to live in it.

...than live with love

see the endless sea,
feel the sound
 Rippling along tired overhead lines
      ease
      into a time without form
      void
      darkness upon the face of the deep.

7
**what would it cost me
to base a character on her ?**

8
be smart! - trust me! - you cant spend your life dusting counters
and counting raindrops
staring at computer screens
in the cold

Too shy to ask
too proud to cry
a nice girl
curious,
an aliveness I had not felt in years.
It was complicated
too many questions
what's wrong with the truth?

9
Truth is always a problem.

10
There is no one else to talk to -
talking -
that's when the trouble starts.

11
they cannot even talk
and when his eyes move,
his lips lie
and when he offered a lift he had good reasons -places everyone!
The curtain of your life
is about to rise
and
He should never have let her go.
    the mother so affected, the stance so stiff
    so stiff that everyone was embarrassed
building hopeless hopes -
I felt bad about that.

12
STOP asking
STOP investigating

but I cannot leave
until
I understand what happened here.

13
I could have made him happy
but we never get the lives we wanted
or do we?
choices along the way, odd turns on byways
freewheeling on turnpikes
churning dust on trails
always
a stranger and a pilgrim
always living in a dream.

When people creep up from behind
and their shadow crosses yours
beware
switch off the music,
plant yourself in sand
and hope
your shadow has the strength to create its own reality.

14
the chapter heading reads
WHAT??
Don't hide behind confidentially
whenever it suits you that's just weird and when I re-reread...
it just gets worse -Condemned for loving??
When I re-read the testimony
I knew
this was not good.

15
was there concrete

credible evidence?

ANYTHING that doesn't condemn him?

crumbling, terse messages
communication gone wrong
people always seeing things through their own filter - their OWN filter.
Don't take the blame for a conversation overheard

words words words words
personal views/their views/her views his views/panoramic views/heady views

just not my views and NOT my intentions.

16
Stand still and see your **salvation**
and remember
between you and them
stands a shield
as large as the universe
and a million times more strong.
Nothing
can be as bad as the unread pages
your shadows have cast.

17.
anonymous letters
lost letters
to lost ones

why does The Bad always seem
to be the interpretation
of my way
that somehow
what I speak is wrong,
unjust/bad timing/short
its not

its just not.

18
don't turn things around on me
Don't you think the notes are important
in my office
in the encyclopedia
I'm NOT THIS PERSON
you claim me to be.
white envelopes fall
threats
clothing and quills
the door said open
but the face said closed.

19
OK **OK**
I'm going
quitting the drama
it will be good for me anyway
I need to unpack this excess baggage others have loaded me - too
many tomorrows.
The producer said
fight for your life -
it's the credits RUN!
it's a paranormal adventure, back to the future and meetings of an
uncommon kind.

# 90

20
All this,
preempted by fee notes
and choices made
while collecting information

      the isolated house
was a gift
after the chaos of questions which could not be answered.
Remember:
Glass offers no protection in gunfire
and ink spills
don't come out

21
it was the slow pace
language drawn as the first weapon in conflict.

such deliberateness
makes the heart beat fast
in anticipation of what is to come.

22
Tell you what:
dazzle them with basics
the corner stones of civilization
we'll work together though our theories are different.

Peeking in,
it looked like **they** would get along while supper waited and tummies
rumbled on an endless light train through clouds of waste and
unknown terrain.

Go play the piano yesterday
like you did today -
there is **much** to practice and time is brief
on tennis courts with short volleys -

a mosaic of faces

[best looking facing forwards]
and in slow motion
all shots are, well,
S

    l

       o

          w.

A reading of the poem
Ode to The Unfinished Book
At the opening of

Letters to Spring
(A solo exhibition by Cheryl Penn).
(Cheryl Penn and Esther Stein)
31st August 2019

EXISTIR

Não quero pensar.
Quero deixar a vida
fluir
sem a consciência
do ar que respiro;
quero ser urn poema
não escrito nem sonhado
ou ser os olhos
que me vêem sem
sentir esta náusea
diluida em verso.
Depois me dirão
para que me obrigaram
a Exisitr!

Teresinka Pereira

EXISTIR

No quiero pensar
Quiero dejar la vida
fluir
sin la conciencia
del aire que respiro.
Quiero ser un poema no escrito,
no soñado
o ser los ojos
que me pueden ver
sin sentir esta náusea
Diluida en verso.
Después vengan a decirme
ipara qué me han forzado
a existir!

Teresinka Pereira

TO EXIST

I don't want to think.
I like to leave life
to flow
without conscience
of the air I breeze.
I want to be a poem
not written nor dreamed
or to be the eyes
that see me without
fccling this nausea
diluted in verse.
Then you will tell me
why you made me
to exist!

Teresinka Pereira

International Writers & Artists
Teresinka Pereira, Pres.
PO Box 352048
Toledo, OH 43635-2048
USA

POEMS TANKA

The man of vision
Conquered by illusion
Looks to the stars
Dreaming that elsewhere
Some eyes are staring at him.

Keepers of all fights they come
With a weird vademecum
To the newborn child
That decisive moment
Must draw a destiny.

Our footsteps
Across the sand of memories
Are stolen by the wave.
There will always be other
Footsteps caught in a dreamland.

Nadia-Cella Pop

Arpad Šalamon
3210 KONJICE
Aškerčeva 4
SLOVENIJA

Recollection

75 and I'm still alive Who
could would have thot
Here is a list of everyone
I was going to become
That's right First No one
Idler than fuck Idle set
on stuck O. K. No train
coming I can stay here
forever Which means
as long as I want Only
what's to want Last time
I wanted something it
just didn't work out Now
I don't even remember
what it was I wanted
Fair enough A good thing
is to keep the first person
out of things Like writing
Staying in the first person
just keeps things messy
Like you care When that's
not true I can't remember
the last time I knew or
cared about anything true
True just keeps changing
Into something otherwise
Is that hard to imagine
Forgetting makes things
easier And truer That I can
remember Maybe Do you
think I can remember me
Only barely Here is truly
what there is Sky is sky
Ground is ground Get
around much Not really

Saleh

Sherarts

NONAPTYCH 8

A non-descript man steps before
The display window of a health aids store
And gazes with thoughtful demeanor
Upon the wide variety of insect repellants,
Poisons, sprays, the scourge of the insect kingdom
With the curse of pestilence and sheer bother
Ever present. Deep in meditation.
A happy smile drifts across his lips
Such a plethora of remedies for the infestation
That infect the earth, that crowd the earth,
Such business models that propel commercial
Ventures as these are most praiseworthy
And well deserve the approbation of the public.
He, self-contained, the theme of eradication of
The vile life force, is the theme that he is
Obsessed by, that tills him with a feeling of
Contentment in the insecure place he inhabits,
That there IS something he can depend upon
In this world of insecurity and dread tempests
That dwell upon the land. These elixirs are no
Surprise to him as he possesses
A multiplicity of them, collecting them as any
Enthusiast would in the battleground of life,
To wipe out the infestations that envelope him
And other inhabitants of the loathsome cities.
Yes! He smiles and clucks inwardly
At the sight of the weapons against
The insect hordes and their larger affinities
Of higher orders of vile orders of life.
He is armed and ready to proceed against
The enemies of the commonweal. Such is
The underlying basis of his joy, his hopeful

Air, his purposeful glint in the eye that
Animates his step as he walks along Queens
Boulevard to the hardware emporium
Where he parks himself and again is,
Window shopping for insecticides of greater
Volume contained in huge canisters with
Appropriate warnings in bold red print
And skull and bones motifs, the word POISON
Underlined, dire warnings on use.
Such danger warnings add to the sheer
Excitement that vibrates within him:
He admires, adores, reveres these commercial
Endeavors that defend the public against
The pestilences that threaten it. He walks a narrow path
As he strolls the boulevard with measured stride,
His mind enraptured by the visual display of
The countermoves of the forces that constitute
The counterattack of the commonweal.
He, himself, knows a sense of fulfillment,
A sense of security, serenity and a deep, inherent
Joy, kept hidden from observers
As he strolls on Queens Boulevard, at one
With the people, none could sense the
Strength of his passion, the severity of
His mordant obsessions, the height of
His mirth at the thought of the
Crushing blow he entertains upon
The vile phalanxes that would
Bring the world to destruction.
The means of counterstroke lie within the
Grasp of the defenders. Oh! The havoc
wrought by these will be something to behold as
it reveals itself in its broad dimensions.
His little servant squirts about in his mind

Dropping little hints of biochemical joy.
He is self contained in his walk.
None walking near him could guess
At the sheer inhumanity of his inner
Thoughts, the perverted notions that
Drift through his mind, the cynical
Misanthropy that crash violently on
The naked shore as he paces forward
As a well dressed burgher of the city
Of magnificent sway.
How could they divine it?
He is very normal looking,
Most sedate, harmless even.
But he is not. A force resides within him.
A streak of hatred invisible to those around him.
Hail to the bug spray, to the chemical buckets
That threaten disaster
To the grave distempers of our time.
The micro and macro combat measures
 That add a spice of life to
This new warfare, Those passing by will
Never perceive in this very ordinary man
Who walks by them harmless and unthreatening.
Who ever would suspect him
Of bearing within himself such
Violent urges. And yet they are there!
He knows his own mind and the vile world
Around him. He will begin slowly but with a solid plan
To combat the insect world and cleanse the streets
Of the metropolis, ridding it of the infection
That forever possesses it, enraptures it.
He is pledged to overturn the infamy
And to place the city in a mode of salvation
That will free it at last from the rot of destruction.

NONAPTYCH 9

Does serenity arrive after a storm?
Does tranquility come after a tirade?
As he sits in leisurely stillness
His body seemingly purged of ill temper
He reflects on his misanthropy,
His disgust for the world around him
That destructive tendency that dominates
His world view into a total negativity
Can any good come of this?
He doesn't care. He must void his disgust
And rage in any way he can.
In the present he has voided his ill feelings,
His temper is assuaged
In his chair overlookimg Queens Boulevard.
He is quietly reflective, meditating
Upon the spew that has come out of him.
The rage has dissipated and a calmness
Has taken hold of him. A tactical forbearance
Now rests upon him. He now wants only
To breathe and sit in a serene restiveness
As the day drifts slowly by, but well he knows
That he is likely to explode again but now
He lacks the energy for it. He lazily observes
Passers-by on the other side of Queens Boulevard,
The "boulevard of death." A restful languor
Falls upon him. He has not the energy
To fulminate against the powerful forces
That dominate the world. He longs only to breathe
Softly in the lazy afternoon of torpor
That rests upon him, bringing him into a mellowness.
Can it really be that his conception of the world
Is as cruel and terrible as he proclaimed it recently?

Upon reflection, Yes. His opinions have not altered.
It is only that he is tired and
Lacks the energy to carry on with it
So he is quiescent for now but
The internal shouting will come forward
Once more within the confines of his mind.
The world does not change because of a lack
Of energy residing in his body on a temporary basis.
His mind knew the truth of his assertions.
He will not weaken and become flaccid. He knows
He is right and the hatred is still there. Looking
Out over the boulevard, he watches
The long rows of cars and trucks in their
Endless columns going east and west,
Without rhyme or reason, upon the asphalt
And concrete of meaninglessness. Really,
Really, there is nothing here that commands attention,
That requires insight or contemplation.
It is simply the slow progression towards death.
He knows this as surely as anybody does. It is a cold
Day in autumn. The sun shines brightly
But yet nothing illumes the soul of the multitudes
Who move relentlessly on their paths
of unthinking blankness.
The tidal waves of roaches move ever forward
In their ludicrous progressions
Towards nothing. The joke is on them
In their earnestness of movement, as if
There were some point to it all.
There isn't any. There's no purpose to any of it.
The movements are delusional
Like everything is. Colonies of ants and spiders
Move onwards with a purposelessness that has
No substance, no basis. Like some entomologist

Studying an ant heap, cataloguing the strange
Movements that defy human understanding,
He idly watches the obscene tides
Of the enslaved creatures.
Observe, yes, by all means, but do not flatter yourself,
That it all amounts to anything of note.
The world goes on and on in its pointless
Exhibitionism. Why do people take it all so seriously
When clearly it amounts to nothing at all.
But they must make the motions of finding
Meaning in their lives when there is none,
following instincts driven into their tiny minds.
Seated on this high vantage point
He is more sure of that than ever.
In this high perch, in this cat bird seat
He sees the insignificance of it all.
What could be clearer than that?
A serenity falls upon him from this height.
He does not hear the sounds from the traffic
Or the streets, only his own monotonous breathing
And the occasional puff of hot air
Coming from the radiators
And yes, the sound of his breathing
With a predictable regularity.
But for the occasional movement of
His legs, the turn of his eyeballs,
A solemn stillness holds forth. He is trapped
Here in this observational post
High above the boulevard below,
Forced to view the layout of life below
Down in the caverns of the vast, mysterious streets,
and the troglodytic hordes that infest them,
who meander about in the preordained patterns,
Cast down for them from on high.

Arnold Skemer

Plague!
ExTincTion
Re-Creation
SKOLNICK
2018

CITADEL 111/12

Shadowlands
infused with iron
a sail through
steel moats
Jasmine dares
progressions,
hollow barriers
of meaning sewn
on foreheads
visions of bose
bottles of a
chrome nickel
solution,
voiceprints startled
a congress of crows
in the smoggy evil
sky brazed by antique
pedigrees. Upstairs
shelves of packaged
potions await arrest.

       ***

Items on the list;
a forgotten breath,
hyenas at the gate,
the scaffold spectators,
xylophone sounds,
demotions,
famine, a
blended utterance,
the adumbration
of untergehen.

       ***

Long night restraints
crossed barricades of
wooden splints,
gargantuan tombs
purchased with
gold fillings,
pounds of certified
meat preserved in
bottles with artificial
accolades. Distribution
of goods: manacles and
candles, bugle scores
composed on secure phone
Lines, miocenic reports
grizzled with photons
and powdered broth,
ninety nine point nine
nine percent pure.
***

4/1/18

Stone

CITADEL 111/17

A skillet operator
a door closes a
spectacle of silence
night sentences
beyond synchronous
trial posts heckled
fables evening
fissures the witnesses
fled. We ate at a diner
along the way, the
whistle of the night
express. Sounds clock
hounds grasp planks
corroded in society
in the long corridor
for execution after
the clamor fainted
crippled antecedents
plunged from ancient
soil. Charts blood
swallows all evening.
Uneven ears listen
for the basenji's
silence claws reign
(Spinozistic spangled
cases assigned to
the ledger). Dress
codes, gold and brass,
gaming tables.
***
A flux of doctrines
fables flight registers
miscalibrated clocks
blaring bugles snakes
evicted from the zoo

fugitives plots pleas
birth injuries cured
by the sea. The water
tower smoked a xylophonic
note savored the sail
recognized on a rail.
***

Harpsichord sounds
sensations of survival
cold gunfire
theatrical applause
fate eyes palmprints
doctrines in the
pasted night.
***

Gauges
sutures
frames
messengers of death
a slight delay in the
farther estate the
fiddle the stamp pledged
bridges collapse dissolve
in the tundra where the
blue bus sails into space
feeds ideas into Husserlian
ground ideas felt severed
from bloody events hollowed
in Nuremberg nourished in
Leuven calibrated adumbrated
rattled in ruins explained
in tranquil blazes. Gottschalk's
western flank taunted a dream
nabbed enumerated wrapped in
steel ribbon known by evicted
bone recognized by 86.5%
facial reconstruction.
***

Stone

CITADEL 111/49

Geistboards transfered
grieved and ridiculed
in the dismal air
Engulfed, named on
a list, analyzed,
enforced rips
and riots, fil-
tered shoe sound
clatter down
buoyant steps
into Plato's
scorched tunnel.
***

The ambassador rip-
ples pardons, rows
of particles de-
parted, sutures of
death bought claws
and remnants, snow
fell worse than
thought brought
torches over mil-
lions of hobbling
carts shearing
life after the
war's end. Blind,
withered soldiers
found in the yards
of clamor.
***

The principal menace:
a switch is pulled;

the train crosses a
barrier. I fail to
comprehend the light
of Oz Park. Undiscovered
gadgets plop into the
summit. Ideologies baffle
citizens, pardon fashions,
hustle armies, smoke miles
of cigarettes, wave goodnight
for the trillionth time
and brief folios criss-
crossed with hunger.
  ***

2/25/19

Marilyn Stone

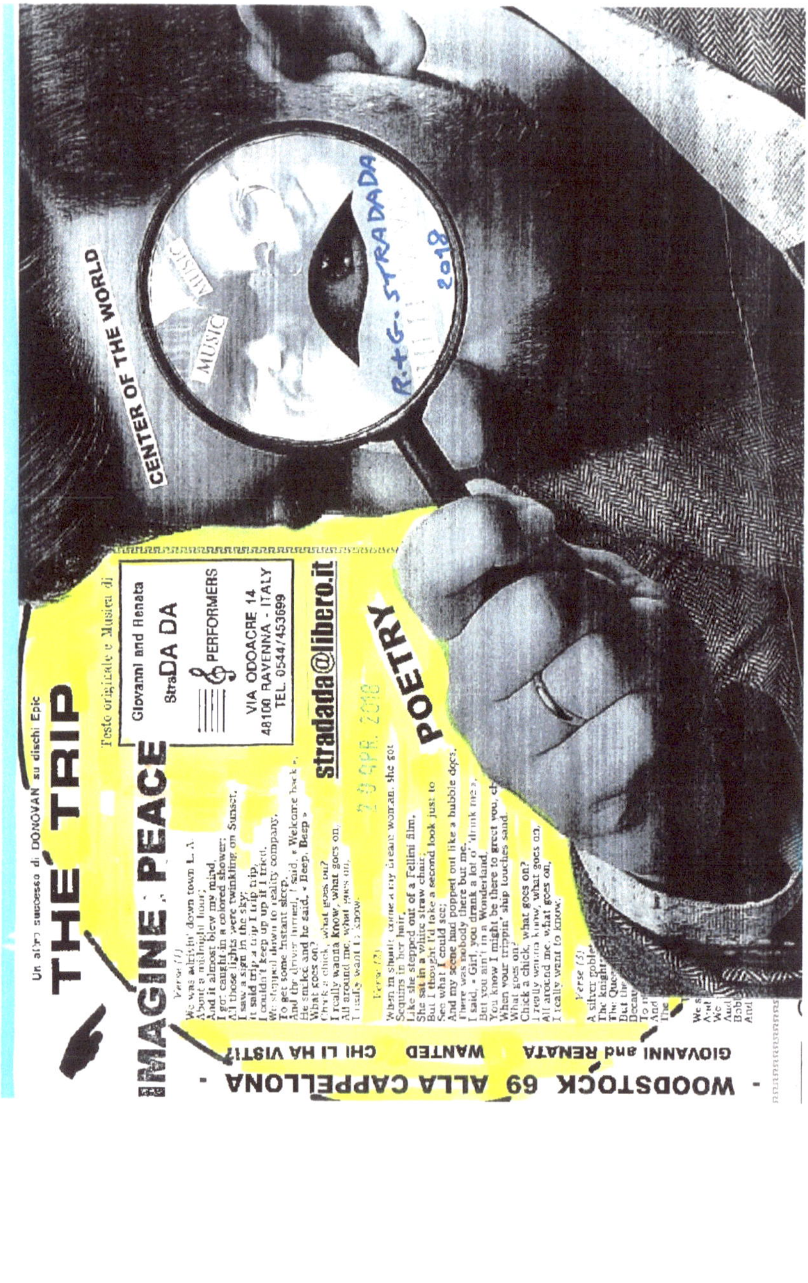

THE TRIP

Un altro successo di DONOVAN su dischi Epic

IMAGINE : PEACE

Testo originale e Musica di

Giovanni and Renata

StraDA DA

PERFORMERS

VIA ODOACRE 14
48100 RAVENNA - ITALY
TEL. 0544/453699

stradada@libero.it

POETRY

CENTER OF THE WORLD

MUSIC MUSIC

R.+G. STRADADA 2018

2 0 APR. 2018

- WOODSTOCK 69 ALLA CAPPELLONA - GIOVANNI and RENATA WANTED CHI LI HA VISTI?

Verse (1)
We was adrivin' down town L.A.
About a midnight hour;
And it almost blew my mind,
I got caught in a colored shower;
All those lights were twinkling on Sunset,
I saw a sign in the sky;
It said trip a trip I trip trip,
I couldn't keep up up if I tried.
We stepped down to reality company,
To get some instant sleep.
And the driver turned, I said, « Welcome back »,
He smiled and he said, « Beep, Beep »
What goes on?
Chick a chick, what goes on?
I really wanna know, what goes on,
All around me, what goes on,
I really want to know.

Verse (2)
When in shuffle come a my dream woman, she got
Sequins in her hair,
Like she stepped out of a Fellini film,
She sat in a white straw chair;
But I thought I'd take a second look just to
See what I could see;
And my scene had popped out like a bubble does,
There was nobody there but me.
I said, « Girl, you drank a lot o' 'drink me »,
But you ain't in a Wonderland,
You know I might be there to greet you, ch
When your trippin' ship touches sand.
What goes on?
Chick a chick, what goes on?
I really wanna know, what goes on,
All around me, what goes on,
I really want to know.

Verse (3)
A silver goblet
The knight
The Quee
But the
Becau
To
And
The

frigid water (-
Verburg
4/13/16

THE DESIGN:
paid in cash.
Verbung

LA PORTE DU MONDE: **DU RÊVE**   poème de Guido Vermeulen

Ankh
Guido

ТЕЧЕНИЕ БЕРЕМЕННОСТИ, РОДОВ
Дата, час
Состояние
ZUROMSKAS

Дата	Общее состояние	Состояние молочных желез	Высота дна матки	Лохия	мочев. пузыря	кишеч-ника	Назначения

9 789389 690880